COFFEE

·BREAK·

WRITING

METRO BOOKS
New York

An Imprint of Sterling Publishing Co., Inc.
1166 Avenue of the Americas
New York, NY 10036

ISBN 978-1-4351-6932-6

For information about custom editions, special sales, and premium
and corporate purchases, please contact Sterling Special Sales
at 800-805-5489 or specialsales@sterlingpublishing.com.

Manufactured in China

2 4 6 8 10 9 7 5 3 1

sterlingpublishing.com

Design: John Gillard
Image Credits: see page 176

COFFEE ·BREAK· WRITING

100 prompts for inspired writing on the go

JOHN GILLARD

METRO BOOKS
New York

CONTENTS

INTRODUCTION

With the time constraints of a busy life, it can be hard to find those important moments in which to sit back, relax, and let your creativity flow. This book encourages you to make the most of those snippets of time when taking a break from the hectic rhythms of modern life. Many of the exercises in this book are designed to be completed in the time it takes you to finish your macchiato.

Some exercises encourage you to write with freedom, others require careful observation; some are simple, others challenging. What they all have in common is that they allow a release of imagination and creativity, and get the pen flowing across the page. There is something about this process, as your mind meanders and sparks, that can bring magic to the page.

While allowing you to simply relax and enjoy the act of writing, the exercises promote key elements of storytelling and idea generation. Characterization, texture of language, brevity, rhythm, and tone of prose are just some of the core elements covered. There are occasional exercises dedicated to great writers of the twentieth century, as well as occasional quotes to offer inspiration and an insight into their literary magic.

Great writing is about creating compelling and believable characters with authentic voices and in locations that can immerse the reader—even if it is just a very short piece within the micro-world of your coffee break. And who knows where your thoughts and ideas will take you? Perhaps out of the coffee shop or office, or off the park bench, and into an entirely new world which has not yet been created...

HOW TO USE THIS BOOK

The book is formed of single-page and double-page exercises. You can pick and choose which exercises you want to work with; there is no defined order in which to approach them. Dip in however you like, or start at the beginning and work through to the end.

The single-page exercises can be completed in a very short amount of time whereas the double-page spreads vary in complexity. You can complete any of the exercises in your own time, coming back to them or taking notes and ideas away with you for future use. Alternatively, you might like the challenge of completing each one within your coffee break. Some exercises will ask you to finish in the time it takes you to drink your coffee or reach the end of the page!

Each exercise begins with a title and directions on how to proceed. Often you will be directed to tackle the exercise step-by-step and using the boxes and rule lines provided. You might be asked to make notes, compose similes, generate story ideas, jot down a character profile, create textured descriptions, have fun with word play, or simply let loose upon the page.

You will often be provided with further instructions or guidance in the form of colored boxes. These might help your approach or simply offer an interesting snippet of information. There are also quotes from famous writers offering inspiration, which relate directly to the content of the exercise.

Feel free to use the book however best suits you. Take it with you on your coffee breaks, sit down, relax, grab a coffee, open up one of the pages, and lose yourself in your words. Have fun and let it flow!

 **01**

COFFEE-BREAK BEAT

Grab a coffee, sit down, have a look around you, and choose an object. Once you've had a sip of coffee, write down the name of the object you have chosen and follow it with a description, or any thoughts or connotations triggered by the object. Write without too much thought or pondering. Allow the words to hit the page, however random or unconstructed they might be.

CONTINUE THIS PROCESS

In between each sip of coffee, cast your eyes somewhere around you and write a few words about what you see. Continue in this way, forming a continuous paragraph across this page and the next as you sip your coffee. By the time you have finished your drink you will have an intriguing insight into the environment surrounding you, written to the beat of your coffee break.

"Coffee is a lot more than just a drink; it's something happening. Not as
in hip, but like an event, a place to be, but not like a location, but like
somewhere within yourself. It gives you time, but not actual hours or
minutes, but a chance to be, like be yourself, and have a second cup."

Gertrude Stein, Selected Writings *(1946)*

PERSONIFICATION

Giving human attributes to everyday objects can make them really leap off the page. You can use this impact to create both fun and meaningful descriptions. Follow the steps below to create this personification of objects.

STEP-BY-STEP

1. In the first box, make a list of adjectives that can describe a person, e.g., obnoxious.

2. In the second box, make a list of random objects and things, e.g., ice cream.

3. In the final box, pair these adjectives and nouns together, e.g., a bowl of obnoxious ice cream.

HUMAN ADJECTIVES

RANDOM OBJECTS

HUMAN ADJECTIVES/RANDOM OBJECTS

EXTREME YOU

NUANCES

We all have many sides and nuances to our personality. It can be a great source of inspiration to use these various elements, take them to extremes, and let them run wild. We can create many interesting characters this way, and we will naturally have ideas about what makes each character tick.

Write down some of the character traits and idiosyncrasies you possess; include both subtle and obvious ones. These might be optimism, occasional anxiety, or a penchant for a nibble of cheese for supper—leading sometimes to nightmares. They might make for interesting starting points for a new character.

In the box below, take these traits and idiosyncrasies and give a character name to each of them, the location where they live, how they dress, and finally what makes them tick. What are their desires and aspirations?

HAIKU

04

Construct two or three haiku on the opposite page that can connect to make a longer poem. Below is an example of a modern haiku, a collection by American writer Nick Virgilio. Haiku themes are traditionally based on nature, the seasons, and human nature. Virgilio merged these themes with grittier ones such as his urban surroundings and the death of his brother in the Vietnam War.

lily:
out of the water...
out of itself

evening sun
on the back of the bullfrog:
dragonfly

the young leaves blown
this way, that way
spring moon

deep in rank grass,
through a bullet-riddled helmet:
an unknown flower

flag-covered coffin:
the shadow of the bugler
slips into the grave

Vietnam monument
mirroring cherry blossoms
and gold star mothers

a blind musician
extending an old tin cup
collects a snowflake

shadowing hookers
after dark:
the cross in the park

silent World Series:
deaf mutes arguing over
the play at the plate

Nick Virgilio, Selected Haiku (1985)

RHYTHM AND BEAT

Haiku is a form of poetry that originated in Japan in the seventeenth century. It is written to a beat: the rhythm of a haiku is generally five beats for the first line, seven beats for the second line, and five beats for the third line. These beats are usually the syllables of the words in a line, with the middle line of the three usually being the longest, but not necessarily. In the penultimate haiku in the example above, Virgilio has a shorter middle line: "after dark." The colon acts as a measure for the beat—which is silence—a pause, before the final line begins. This is the work of a highly attuned haiku poet but highlights the idea that haiku is a feeling of a beat rather than overly prescriptive. It can, however, be helpful to use the prescriptive method of five, seven, five syllables per line to begin with.

THEMES

You might like to choose one or all of the traditional haiku
themes of nature, the seasons, and human nature, and perhaps
bring in some of your own themes in the vein of Virgilio.

FLAVOR MEMORY

Do you have a memory of a taste you have never forgotten? It may be a memory you would rather forget or one that fills you with joy. Write a few lines below describing this flavor and where it was that you tasted it.

"As I ate the oysters with their strong taste of the sea and their faint metallic taste that the cold white wine washed away, leaving only the sea taste and the succulent texture, and as I drank their cold liquid from each shell and washed it down with the crisp taste of the wine, I lost the empty feeling and began to be happy and to make plans."

Ernest Hemingway, A Moveable Feast *(1964)*

Below, try to bring this flavor memory into a fictitious context. For example, might it be the last taste experience of an inmate on death row, or a taste that conjures up memories of lost love to a character?

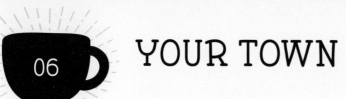

YOUR TOWN

Write a description, in four sentences, of the city, town, or village where you are right now. Within the four sentences, bring in the four senses of sound, smell, taste, and touch. What does your city sound like? What smells are unmistakably linked to your town—is it the freshly baked dough of a bagel bar or the scent of seaweed in the air?

WORD ASSOCIATIONS

07

Write down what you mainly associate with each of the words below, in one or two sentences:

HOME

CUBA

WHALES

CAFÉ

DOWNPOUR

STREAM OF CONSCIOUSNESS

Write a stream of consciousness for ten minutes—or until you reach the end of the page or your coffee, whichever comes first—triggered by the quote below.

{
"Please accept my resignation. I don't want to belong to any club that will accept people like me as a member."

Groucho Marx, Grouch and Me *(1959)*
}

WORD PROGRESSION

Underneath the words "coffee" and "break" below, write a continuous list of words, each one associated in some way with the previous one. Do this until you reach the thick gray line. Underneath the line, write a sentence that incorporates the words "coffee" and "break," as well as the last word from each of your lists.

Following on from this initial sentence, continue to write until you reach the end of the page, opposite or until you have finished your coffee break.

COFFEE   BREAK

Coffee-break word progression complete!

UNEXPECTED SIMILES

On the page opposite, form some new, unexpected comparisons to replace the common similes below.

As fast as a speeding bullet

As grumpy as a bear with a sore head

As honest as the day is long

As old as the hills

As high as a kite

As cool as a cucumber

COFFEE-BREAK LINE

11

Certain coffee shops ask for the customer's name, to write it onto the cup. Imagine a scenario where the name on the cup prompts some interaction between the customer and barista, or perhaps somebody else in the line. Write the dialogue that ensues, a very short story, or a plotline for a longer piece.

LISTEN OUT

If you frequent a coffee shop that asks for your name, then you could listen out for the names of those in front of you for inspiration.

JACK

12 THE GREAT INDOORS

Ernest Hemingway, one of the twentieth century's most influential writers, was a great lover of the outdoors. Much of his work was influenced by his adventures: *The Old Man and the Sea* was inspired by his love of sailing and fishing; *For Whom the Bell Tolls* was about the Spanish Civil War, in which he was heavily involved. He was equally at home indoors, sipping whiskey, chatting to friends, and writing. This exercise is inspired by what can sometimes seem like two different worlds—the great outdoors and, indeed, the great indoors.

OBJECTS AND THEMES

List four objects that are in your current surroundings.
If you are indoors, list what is around you. Then either
look through a window or imagine what might be outside.
If you are outdoors, then list what is around you and
imagine what might be inside a nearby building.

INSIDE
1 _____
2 _____
3 _____
4 _____

OUTSIDE
1 _____
2 _____
3 _____
4 _____

INSIDE-OUT

Write a short piece—whether it be a poem, flash fiction,
a very short story, or stream of consciousness—to include
some or all of the inside and outside words in your list.

"But if the light was gone in the Luxembourg I would walk
up through the gardens and stop in at the studio apartment
where Gertrude Stein lived at 27 rue de Fleurus."

Ernest Hemingway, A Moveable Feast (1964)

ALLITERATION

1 Write a list of random objects, people, and places next to the bullet points below.

2 Describe each of them along the dotted lines using just two or three words, but with each descriptive word beginning with the same letter.

3 Write a paragraph incorporating some or all of the alliterations you have created. Alliteration can create rhythm, mood, and poetic lyricism.

"His soul swooned slowly as he heard the snow falling faintly through the universe and faintly falling, like the descent of their last end, upon all the living and the dead."

James Joyce, Ulysses (1922)

WORLD CITIES

Write down three cities of the world, followed by a single sentence to describe each one.

Choose one of the cities (the one you found most interesting to describe) and write a short piece in which you "talk" to the city as if you were talking to a person.

MUSICAL INSPIRATION

Write in a stream of consciousness style while listening to music. Let your observations and ideas flow from your pen across the page as you listen. Allow the lyrics and rhythm of the songs to inspire you consciously with their words and ideas, or subconsciously through connotations and the feelings they evoke. Write until you have filled the pages.

"Everything in the universe has a rhythm,
everything dances."

Maya Angelou

SELF-IMPOSED CONSTRAINTS

EXPERIMENTAL

The French writing collective Oulipo (formed in 1960) is a group of experimental writers who place constraints on their work. An example of a constraint is the "lipogram," where the writer must compose a piece of writing with a letter from the alphabet missing. One of the greatest Oulipo writers, Georges Perec, produced an entire novel without using the letter "e." The book, *A Void* (1969), was not only fully coherent, but used the idea of the missing "e" to represent the author's missing parents, who were killed in the Holocaust.

"A gap will yawn, achingly, day by day, it will turn into a colossal pit, an abyss without foundation, a gradual invasion of words by margins, blank and insignificant, so that all of us, to a man, will find nothing to say."

Georges Perec, A Void (1969)

Can you set up an Oulipo approach to a short piece of writing, using a lipogram that relates in some way to the story? It's a big challenge, but it can be rewarding. For example, a woman is playing roulette with her last twenty dollars. She attempts to place it all on the number 20. The story has no letter "t." The twentieth letter of the alphabet is missing, and so too is the number 20 on the roulette table...

KILLER OPENING

{
"As Gregor Samsa awoke one morning from uneasy dreams he found himself transformed in his bed into a gigantic insect."

Franz Kafka, The Metamorphosis *(1915)*
}

Above is the opening line to Franz Kafka's novella *The Metamorphosis*. Can you come up with some first lines of potential stories that pack a huge punch? The intrigue and shock might serve to frame an entire story.

Fill the pages below and opposite with as many killer opening lines as you can think of. You don't need an entire story to be laid out in front of you. Let your mind scan potential characters, episodes, and scenarios that might shock and intrigue. You can mine ideas from the world around you, from the local environment in which you are sitting right now, or from the wider world. Let your mind wander and see if any sparks fly. Let characters introduce themselves and episodes explode onto the page. Story ideas can start with the smallest of seeds that pack a big punch.

_____
_____
_____
_____
_____
_____
_____
_____
_____
_____
_____
_____
_____
_____
_____
_____
_____
_____

INSPIRATION

"The first line almost knocked me off the bed. I was
so surprised…I thought to myself that I didn't know
anyone was allowed to write things like that."

Gabriel García Márquez, on the opening line of Kafka's
The Metamorphosis

LET THE MIND WANDER

Look around you for ten to twenty seconds, pick up your pen, and write. Write with a zoned-out, blank mind. Whichever words come out of you, run with them. Write with this same approach until you reach the end of the next page. Do not worry about grammar or spelling. Simply see where your mind takes you.

 **19**

FOUR SEASONS, FIVE SENSES

Write down words you associate with the four seasons, via the five senses (see opposite, below). You could do this from your own perspective, or that of an imagined character.

WINTER

SPRING

SUMMER

FALL

FIVE SENSES
Sight, hearing, taste, smell, touch

20 COMPASS POINTS

Write the inner thoughts of four people, all looking up to the sky at the same moment in time but separated by their location. One person is in the northwest, one is in the southeast, and so on. They can be at these different points of orientation in the same house, or the same city or country, or in the four corners of the world. You decide. Use the four spaces framed by the compass below to write their thoughts.

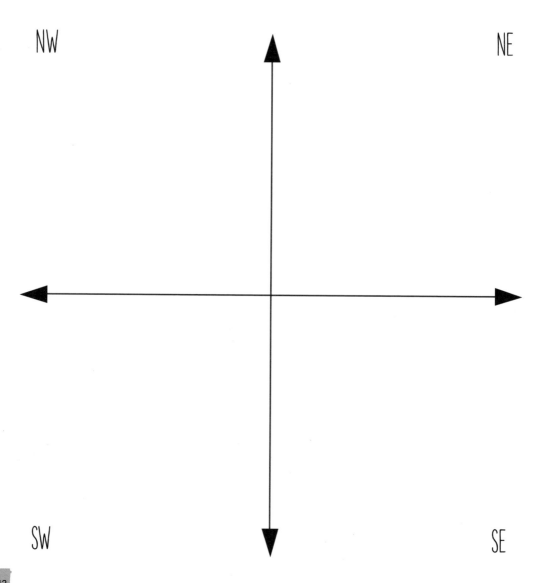

NW

NE

SW

SE

21 BAD INTERVIEW

Write a dialogue between an interviewer and interviewee, in which the interview goes horribly wrong, perhaps with comical effect. What job is at stake? Who are the protagonists? What kind of characteristics do they have? What might happen, or be said, that makes the interview go so wrong?

MIDNIGHT THOUGHTS

22

Use zeugma (see opposite) to compose a sentence or two that describe how you, or an imagined character, might feel during each period of the day, from morning to midnight.

Your character might be someone who ponders life as they drift off to sleep, struggles to start the day, is swamped with work in the afternoon, and socializes in the evening. In the morning, at breakfast, they might feel like this: "My eggs are like my head before coffee—scrambled."

MORNING

AFTERNOON

ZEUGMA

Zeugma is a device whereby a single word refers to two different parts of a sentence, such as "I ate both my lunch and my words."

EVENING

BEDTIME

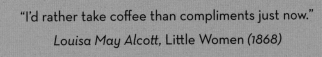

"I'd rather take coffee than compliments just now."
Louisa May Alcott, Little Women (1868)

VIEWING CHARACTERISTICS

Write a short piece in which two characters are close enough that we can see minor details through their eyes. You could write the piece from the perspective of an omnipresent narrator (they), in first or second person (I, you), and/or with dialogue. When you do offer detailed description, because the context is authentic, make it as colorful and textured as possible.

_____

_____

_____

_____

_____

_____

_____

_____

_____

_____

_____

_____

_____

SMALL SCARS AND EYE COLOR

When we describe a character with specific details, such as hair and eye color, we place an image directly into our reader's mind. It is much more effective to allow the image of a character to evolve in the reader's mind through strong characterization. The imagination can paint a far greater picture than words. As readers, we are often viewing a character from afar, via the narrator.

When we literally view someone from afar, it is hard to see the color of their eyes and a small scar on their cheek. We can, as writers, add new layers to a character with such details, when we are seeing them up close within a scene. If we are sitting opposite someone in real life, or are in an embrace or even a fight at close quarters, we might see specific details of their features. In these cases, there is an honesty and truth to a description of eye color and tiny scars. It is real and in context.

WORDPLAY WIT

A brave and bold junior chef says, "Relax, Chef, 'stressed' is just 'desserts' spelled backward."

Can you think of any wordplay, no matter how nonsensical it may sound? Nonsense can turn into something new and imaginative. You may even come up with something you can use in a piece of writing in the future.

PAIRINGS AND FUSED WORDS

A good way to start is to write a number of words naming or describing what you see around you, or words to describe how you feel.

Then see if any words make sense in any way when spelled backward, or when two words are paired together or fused together, such as:

**"Stoptober"
—a month in which to stop
the consumption of alcohol**

Use the page opposite to play and experiment.

25 SWOOPERS AND BASHERS

"Swoopers write a story quickly, higgledy-piggledy, crinkum-crankum, any which way. Then they go over it again painstakingly, fixing everything that is just plain awful or doesn't work. Bashers go one sentence at a time, getting it exactly right before they go on to the next one. When they're done they're done."

Kurt Vonnegut, Timequake *(1997)*

Write your thoughts on the following two subjects:

Subject 1: What separates true friends from acquaintances?
Subject 2: Can there ever be world peace?

 1 Swooper

_____

_____

_____

_____

_____

_____

_____

_____

_____

_____

_____

_____

_____

TWO METHODS

Aim to fill roughly half a page for each subject. With the first subject, compose each sentence as you would want it to appear if someone were to read it back, with little or no editing required.

With the second subject, write your thoughts down without much regard for spelling or syntax, allowing your ideas to flow quickly and freely as one thought follows another.

2 Basher

DIALOGUE: DIALECT

26

Write a dialogue between two people: one has a very strong regional accent; the other does not. Perhaps it is two people talking in the queue of your local café, or an argument in the street. Think about what they are discussing and how the language changes depending on who is speaking. How can you bring out the regional voice on the page? You might change how certain words are written, so the reader hears their voice on the page.

Below is an example from William Faulkner's film transcript for *Country Lawyer* (1943). Here a lawyer is talking with a man he helps to free:

TOBE: Good mawnin', Judge. Dis here's my wife and daughter.

PARTRIDGE: I didn't know you had a family.

TOBE: I been had one a good while. I jest ain't thought to mention um much.

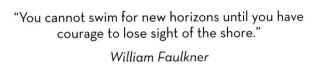

"You cannot swim for new horizons until you have
courage to lose sight of the shore."

William Faulkner

NICKNAMES

In Toni Morrison's award-winning *Song of Solomon* (1977), the main character, Macon Dead III, has the nickname "Milkman," which he acquires because he is breastfed into early boyhood.

Make up some nicknames for characters, with a short explanation as to how they acquired the nickname. You may want to frame this new character name in a sentence, or even write a short episode involving the character. Or, just continue to think of new character nicknames. You may be able to use these at some point in the future, or they may spark an idea for a story. Or, simply enjoy making them up.

WHITE HEAT

28

Take four objects close by you and describe how they feel to touch. Perhaps your first object is your freshly poured coffee. You might start with the sensation of heat, but can you delve deeper? Is it a white piercing heat, or a warming sensation on your palms tempered by the takeout cup's corrugated cardboard sleeve?

29 SUNSET OBSERVATIONS

Imagine you are somewhere observing the setting sun. Describe the light. Where are you in your imagination? How do you feel? What thoughts and memories are triggered?

PING-PONG WRITING

Choose an object and write it down with a full stop after it. Next to it, think of a word which you could consider to be its opposite, counterpart, or variation. For example, "Cell phone. Postcard" (a postcard being a nonelectronic form of communication). Now do the same with "Postcard," for example, "Home" (when you are not on holiday sending a postcard you are at home). Keep batting each word back like a game of ping-pong, creating interesting alternative associations. You might like to then compose a paragraph including some or all of these words?

LIFE'S GREAT PLEASURES

Write an internal dialogue of somebody pondering life's great pleasures. You could bring in the reason why the person is thinking of these positive attributes of life. Maybe he or she is looking for positives to counter a negative moment in life. Or perhaps something that has just occurred has triggered a train of thought, like the first sip of coffee in the morning, or feeling the sun on their face as they close their eyes. Jot down a few ideas briefly in the space below, e.g., stepping on a crisp leaf in the fall.

In the space below, write your own internal dialogue, allowing your thoughts to flow and your ideas to run from one to the next with freedom.

"The morning cup of coffee has an exhilaration about it which the cheering influence of the afternoon or evening cup of tea cannot be expected to reproduce."

Oliver Wendell Holmes Sr.

32

TEAR AWAY!

Gather together some newspapers, magazines, or journals.

Find some words or sentences that interest or intrigue you.

Rip these words and sentences out of the publication(s).

Place the strips in front of you, ready to piece them together.

EMERGING STORY

Piece together the random strips into some kind of cohesive narrative.
Does a story begin to emerge, or perhaps a poem form, story idea,
or character? Use the space below to glue or tape your rearranged
strips, or scribe your newly formed piece of writing.

"You should write because you love the shape of stories and
sentences and the creation of different words on a page."

Annie Proulx

SPARKY TITLE

Write continuously for ten minutes, or until you reach the end of the opposite page or finish your coffee, using the title below as an initial spark.

ONE GAMBLE TOO MANY

MENU BOARD

Look at the menu board on the wall, if you are taking a break in a coffee shop. If not, source a menu from the Internet or imagine one. Replace all of the items on the menu with something else, something completely different. Change the cost of each item to suit the changes you have made. Instead of "Espresso $4/Extra shot $1," you might have "Hitman $2,000/Extra shot $500."

MENU:

ESPRESSO $4

EXTRA SHOT $1

HITMAN $2000

EXTRA SHOT $500

"Who shall I shoot? You choose. Now, listen very carefully: where's your coffee? You've got coffee, haven't you? C'mon, everyone's got coffee! Spill the beans!"

Terry Pratchett, Monstrous Regiment (2003)

THOUGHT-TRAINS

"I urge you: don't cut short these thought-trains of yours.
Follow them through to their end. Your thoughts and your
feelings. Follow them through and you will grow with them."

J. M. Coetzee, Slow Man (2005)

So many ideas can spark and evolve when we lose ourselves in our trains
of thought. Write down a single thought and expand upon it. See where it
takes you, like a runaway train.

LITERAL MEANINGS

Write a dialogue between two people talking on the telephone about a mutual friend, for whose welfare they are concerned. Why are they worried? What has happened to the friend? How does dialogue on the telephone differ from that of face-to-face communication?

CHANGE OF EVENTS

37

You wake up, go to work, have a coffee break at 11 a.m. You have no vacation planned. You want to go home, eat dinner, watch TV, and go to bed. Yet by 10 p.m. you are on a plane. Explain how this change of events came about.

WHAT HAPPENED?
Either make notes for a potential long story or write the story of what happened between coffee break and plane travel.

POST-APOCALYPSE

Imagine you, or a fictional character, are in a post-apocalyptic world where you are the only person remaining in the city, town, or village. Complete the five boxes to build a story and characters.

1　The place where your character is located, e.g., the city/town, building/street, etc.

2　The name and occupation of your character.

3　What has caused the apocalypse?

4 Who else has survived?

5 The first thing your character does, e.g., picks up a phone and dials, walks through the streets...

WHAT HAPPENS NEXT?
By the time you have completed the final box, a story
and characters will have begun to emerge, which you
may like to carry forward into your writing.

39

"THE SECRET OF IT ALL"

> "The secret of it all, is to write in the gush, the throb, the flood, of the moment—to put things down without deliberation—without worrying about their style—without waiting for a fit time or place. I always worked that way. I took the first scrap of paper, the first doorstep, the first desk, and wrote—wrote, wrote...By writing at the instant the very heartbeat of life is caught."

Walt Whitman (1819-1892), the father of free verse

Use your own trigger word, phrase, or thought, and write without pondering or hesitation until you reach the end of the page. Or, use the following line from Whitman as a trigger: "the flood of the moment."

_____

_____

_____

_____

_____

_____

_____

_____

_____

_____

_____

_____

_____

_____

_____

_____

_____

_____

_____

_____

_____

_____

_____

_____

_____

_____

_____

_____

_____

SIPS AND NIBBLES
Momentary sips of coffee or nibbles
on lunch or snacks is allowed!

TECHNOLOGY-FREE MIND

Ensure you have no technology nearby. Sit away from any televisions, put your cell phone in your bag or pocket, store your laptop away from sight.

Shut your eyes for a moment and allow any thoughts about your immediate concerns to float away. Try to replace them with the sounds and smells of your surroundings. Let memories, reflections, and thoughts enter your mind. Or just let your mind become a blank, without the busy rhythms of life flitting in and out.

Breathe in the aroma of your coffee and the sounds of chatter, birdsong, or whatever is around you. Breathe, nice and easy. Let images come in and out of your mind. If something comes into your mind you want to write down—aromas, memories, past vacation locations, colorful images, overheard conversations— then jot it all down in the space below and opposite. If you want to let your pen flow, then do that. Relax and do whatever you want.

41

DISTINCTIVE VOICE

Write a monologue for a character who has a very distinctive way of talking, and who is musing or offering opinions on one of the following subjects (or think of your own):

Religious people preaching
Family members arguing
The price of bread

Politicians lying
What is love?
The meaning of life

BROKEN LANGUAGE

Bring out the character's voice, perhaps using broken language or highfalutin phraseology. Have the spelling, grammar, and cadence mirror the character's delivery. Do they talk in a long, meandering style, with elongated vowel sounds? A sentence structure with lots of subordinate clauses, using colons and semicolons, will serve to mirror this. Short, sharp sentences in clipped English might reflect somebody who stutters and pauses as they talk.

42

LYRICAL NAME

Write a lyrical description of somebody's name so that any feelings about them are mirrored in the language used.

"Lolita, light of my life, fire of my loins. My sin, my soul. Lo-lee-ta: the tip of the tongue taking a trip of three steps down the palate to tap, at three, on the teeth. Lo. Lee. Ta."

Vladimir Nabokov, Lolita (1955)

LITERAL MEANINGS

Write down some objects, professions, and locations below. In as few words as possible, ascribe to each of them their literal meaning, e.g., a doctor is a "health rectifier." In German, a slug is a "naked snail," a *nacktschnecke*.

Write some sentences, or an episode with characters, in which some or all of your literal descriptions can be used. Maybe a character has an affliction and can talk only in literal meanings.

44 FLASH FICTION

ULTRASHORT STORYTELLING

Flash fiction is a form of concise storytelling. Entire stories can be read in the little snippets of free time during our busy lives. It is also possible to compose a fully completed story in just a few coffee breaks, or even just one. Flash fiction is restricted by word count, often fewer than 500 words and as little as six, as in the case of the famous story (often attributed to Ernest Hemingway):

"For sale: baby shoes. Never worn."

A story can be told through a single episode that offers wider connotations, images, ideas, and implied story. A good way in to writing flash fiction is to consider a character that has a very specific problem which they are compelled to overcome. The solution to this problem might be a very specific episode with some compelling action. Start in the middle of this action. If you can, consider a universal human truth, revealed via the characters and action in which we find ourselves embroiled. Then you will have a powerful story to tell.

DEVICES

Stylistically, the key to writing successful flash fiction is brevity: saying as much as possible in as few words as possible. There is no time for lengthy descriptions of people and place, or backstory. It must all be revealed and implied through action, and formulated in the mind of the reader, not on the page. Some devices you could use are:

A twist:
Leading us in one direction and then shifting directions at the end. With a twist, it is important to avoid clichés.

Foreshadowing:
Using imagery to suggest something that is to come, e.g., a small hole in a T-shirt when a gun is involved in the story might imply a character's demise from a fired bullet. A hole in a T-shirt, mentioned in such a short story, will take on real significance. This device—saying a lot in very few words—can be used to great effect.

Universal concepts:
Things that motivate each and every one of us: love, sorrow, pain, longing, desire, hunger, the search for meaning, getting a good night's sleep, finding happiness...Universal themes encourage the reader to contemplate what they have read, adding weight and meaning to the story.

Use the space below to jot down: any story ideas; potential characters; the problem(s) they are compelled to overcome; episodes in the middle, where the action might start; universal concepts you might like to bring into a story. And/or compose a piece of flash fiction.

45

REFLECTIONS

Write the inner thoughts, reflections, and wisdoms of somebody pondering life on their one-hundredth birthday.

WHERE ARE THEY?

Write the centenarian's name, where they live, what family they have around them, and where they are sitting or standing (or in the middle of running a marathon!) when reflecting.

PONDERANCE

In the space below, write the centenarian's reflections and wisdoms.

REVEALING CHARACTER

Write a character profile, including the following facts about them:

CHARACTER PROFILE

Profession:

Where he/she lives:

Marital status:

Height:

Weight/body type:

Hair color:

Eye color:

Medical ailments (if any):

Key family members:

Taking some or all of these facts, write a short piece that reveals them via a narrative or dialogue. Have the facts revealed not by directly mentioning them, but by showing them to the reader through the character's thoughts, words, actions, and other people's interaction with them.

INSPIRATIONAL PHRASE

Use the phrase below as an initial spark to write a short piece, whether it be flash fiction, a poem, or just random thoughts that might lead to further stories and ideas.

THE BOOK ON THE SHELF

48

TRIGGER WORDS

Compose a short piece of writing on the page opposite inspired by the words below:

Complete tranquility

JUXTAPOSITION

Can you take the following mundane tasks and spice them up to create an interesting juxtaposition? It is a useful device, leading readers down an uneventful path, then hitting them with something dramatic or contemplative.

Taking the trash to the recycling unit

Waiting in a queue for a store on Black Friday

Vacuum-cleaning the carpet

Just sitting there, gazing out to sea

HEAVEN, HELL, AND PURGATORY

Write a very brief character profile in each of the sections below, together with a sentence or two explaining why they have reached, or will reach, the category they are in: heaven, hell, or purgatory.

HEAVEN

HELL

PURGATORY

THE TRUE MEANING OF LIFE

51

Write an alternative meaning of life, offered from the musings of a character who has a very different perspective on why we are all here. Perhaps they feel broken by life in some way. Maybe they have a sense of humor about reflections on life, or an overriding competitive streak that sees them trample on others to reach their goals. Perhaps they have psychopathic tendencies...!

THE TRUE MEANING OF LIFE

"We are visitors on this planet. We are here for

100 years at the very most. During that period

we must try to do something good, something

useful, with our lives. If you contribute to

other people's happiness, you will find the true

meaning of life."

14th Dalai Lama

52

SCENARIO PROMPTS

Use one of the prompts below to inspire a piece of writing.
Or make up your own scenario prompt.

Your bag is heavier than when you left it under your desk...

*Something is moving in the trunk of your car, and the car
is stationary...*

*Somebody has just transferred two million dollars into your bank account
with the reference "take it, it's yours"...*

"The fresh smell of coffee soon wafted through the apartment,
the smell that separates night from day."

Haruki Murakami, Colorless Tsukuru Tazaki and
His Years of Pilgrimage *(2013)*

53

CRIME WRITING

Write down a number of potential locations for a crime story. Pick out some key features from those spots, these should be things that set that place apart from anywhere else. Make the locations areas you know intimately. A forensic knowledge of a place is needed when writing crime: because of the nature of a crime, occurring in a given scene, which must be returned to again and again in order for the crime to be solved, the location becomes central. It helps to create the ambience around the story, and even becomes another character—a central character, interweaving stories within a series.

The more detail and texture you can bring, the more the reader will be sucked into the world surrounding the events of your story.

LOCATION

Choose one location and think of a particular street, alleyway, park, beachfront, country track, etc. that you know very well. Write a paragraph describing the location, right down to the textures and shades of stones in a gravel pathway. When a blood-stained claw hammer is found, we want clues as to exactly how long the dry blood that has seeped into the porous gravel has been there. Even if you are not inspired by the crime-writing genre, bringing a location alive with such texture and detail is invaluable.

54   GENERATION X

In modern times there has been a trend in popular culture to assign labels to each generation—from the "Lost Generation" after World War I to "Generation X," who had their formative years through the 1990s; from the "Baby Boomers" of the 1960s to the modern "Millennials."

Think of some new labels of your own for these generations, or for future or previous generations, where a label may have never been assigned. The labels might be comical, apt, cutting, or thought-provoking. You could also use one, some, or all of them within a piece of dialogue, internal monologue, or perhaps your own personal musings.

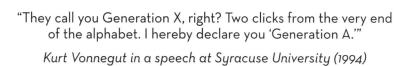

"They call you Generation X, right? Two clicks from the very end of the alphabet. I hereby declare you 'Generation A.'"

Kurt Vonnegut in a speech at Syracuse University (1994)

55 CHANGING TIMES

1. Describe the place where you are sitting right now, or an imagined coffee shop, in two or three sentences.

2. Describe the same place but imagining how it looked in 1930.

3. Imagine how it looked in 1820.

4. Imagine how it looked in prehistoric times.

TODAY

1930

1820

PREHISTORIC

56

DESERTED ISLAND

BLANK PAPER

If you were on a deserted island and had one sheet of blank paper and a pen, what would you write down for posterity? Below is a blank sheet of paper. Place yourself on the island, and write.

57

OBJECT'S TALE

Write a short piece from the perspective of an inanimate object, perhaps a building or an aging coffee-bean grinder found in an antique store. What is its story? What has it seen? Does it have a purpose other than grinding coffee beans? Alternatively, have a character personify an object, so that it comes alive for them, either metaphorically or literally.

58

TASTE MEMORIES

Take a mouthful of your lunch or snack, or sip some of your drink. Write a description of the experience of taste, with any feelings or memories that come to mind. The flavors you experience, and your thoughts while tasting mindfully, may also trigger descriptions of the other four senses: hearing, sight, smell, and touch. Really tap into the experience of tasting your drink or food, and write down everything to the finest detail.

"But, when nothing subsists of an old past, after the death of people, after the destruction of things, alone, frailer but more enduring, more immaterial, more persistent, more faithful, smell and taste still remain for a long time, like souls, remembering, waiting, hoping, on the ruin of all the rest, bearing without giving way, on their almost impalpable droplet, the immense edifice of memory."

Marcel Proust, Swann's Way *(1913)*

AWAKENING THE SENSES

59

Describe the effects of the following on the senses:

WOOD BEING CHOPPED BY AN AX
_____
_____
_____
_____
_____
_____
_____
_____
_____

COFFEE BEANS BEING GROUND TO MAKE AN ESPRESSO
_____
_____
_____
_____
_____
_____
_____
_____

A PLANE TAKING OFF

A CUE BALL BEING STRUCK ON A BILLIARD TABLE AND COLLIDING WITH THE 8-BALL

THE SENSES
How do they sound? Are there any smells that come to mind? Are there any feelings of touch? Are there particular connotations? Are you inside the plane when it takes off or hearing it from afar? Are you chopping the wood?

60 NEW EXPERIENCES

Imagine a child who has never seen snow before. Or a long-term city dweller who has never seen the sea. Write the inner thoughts of one or two people who are experiencing something for the first time. Who are they? How do they describe it? How does it make them feel? What senses and thoughts are aroused in them? Use the possibilities listed below or make up your own.

SNOW   THE DESERT   AN ART GALLERY
THE SEA   FLYING ON A PLANE   EATING AN OYSTER

61 CHARACTER PERSPECTIVES

In the space below, write down three different character types,
e.g., a hostile man.

Think of an incident that might be viewed by a variety of people, such as an
argument in a coffee shop or on a train. Write three different accounts of the
same episode, bringing in the character traits for each narrative, based on the
ones you wrote down.

CHARACTER/EPISODE 1

CHARACTER/EPISODE 2

CHARACTER/EPISODE 3

FINER DETAILS

Look around you, observing the details of your surroundings. Every time you spot something new, write it down, followed by a short description. Keep going until you have scanned the full environment around you.

NEW OBSERVATIONS
We can so often miss the finer details, even in the places we visit most often. Do you see anything that you have not previously observed?

TEXTURE

Adding those extra pieces of detail to our writing
can create texture and enhance the reader's
experience, bringing them further into the
world of our characters.

TEXTURE

Think of some objects that might be corrugated, such as the corrugated cardboard sleeve of a takeout coffee cup. Describe one in detail, putting it into a context within a sentence or paragraph.

For example, "She hesitated to roll the pristine strips of corrugated modelling clay into a ball. And instead ran her fingers down the length of each strip, enjoying its texture."

64 RANDOM WORDS

SEARCH AROUND YOU...

...for random words and/or sentences. Jot them down. These could be stops on a bus timetable, a commercial slogan, or items on a menu. Use the words or sentences to inspire a short passage of writing, whether general musings, lyrical descriptions, snippets of dialogue between fictional characters, or poetry.

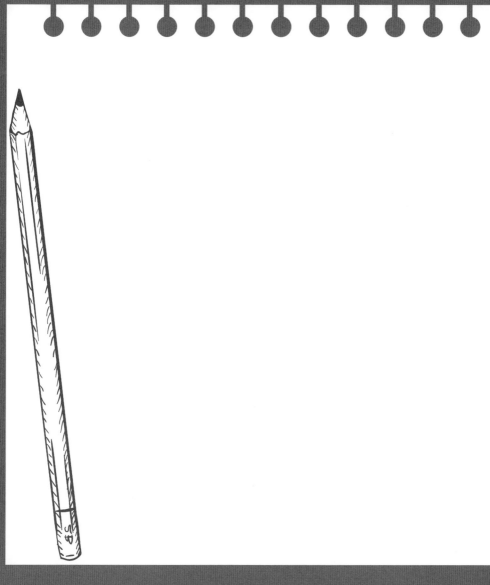

SPECIALIST SUBJECT

65

There is an old adage: write what you know. It is so important to be able to bring honesty, truth, and authenticity to your writing. Choosing a subject that you are passionate about, and have great knowledge of, can help bring these qualities to your work.

Choose a subject you know very well—a hobby, a sport, your work. Make some general notes about the subject in the space below. Note some key words and areas you might cover if you were to explain to somebody else the intricacies of the subject. If you are passionate about gardening, for example, you might note down some of the tools you use, and some of the plants and flowers, compost, and landscaping materials.

Write a story plan, dialogue, or short piece of prose, in which something occurs within the realms and environment of your chosen specialist subject. On the page opposite are some story triggers to help, if needed.

A DARK SECRET

AN UNEXPECTED DISCOVERY

AN UNFORESEEN EPISODE

A CHANGE OF FORTUNE

66 OVERHEARD CONVERSATIONS

Listen out for snippets of conversation around you and note them down in the box below. If you are not able to do this, then search social media to find random sentences from status updates, tweets, posts, etc. If all else fails, then imagine some lines of overheard conversation. Once you have ten to fifteen lines, try to arrange them into cohesive prose. Is there any framework that could help to make sense of any randomness, such as the internal thoughts of people sharing a train carriage?

NOTE-TAKING BOX
For overheard conversation snippets, social media updates, random sentences...

A TRAIN JOURNEY

Imagine a character on a train journey. Describe what your character is looking at as the train speeds along, jolts to a stop, meanders into a station, or crashes! Use sentence length to mirror what you are describing. If your character is looking out of the window at passing scenery, your sentences might be long and flowing, like this example from Flannery O'Connor's "The Train" (1947):

"Now the train was greyflying past instants of trees and quick spaces of field and a motionless sky that sped darkening away in the opposite direction."

MIRRORING

If the action is short and sharp like the train jolting to a stop, or someone on the seat opposite dropping the book they are reading to the floor, the sentences can also be short and sharp.

68

SOBRIQUETS

A sobriquet is a nickname, often given to countries and cities. Change the city sobriquets below, creating unique ones of your own, or think of other cities that lend themselves to unique sobriquets.

BEIJING:
City of Cycles

ROME:
The Eternal City

LOS ANGELES:
City of Angels

OXFORD:
City of Dreaming Spires

NEW YORK:
The Big Apple

QUITO:
City of Eternal Spring

STRAIT OF BAB-EL-MANDEB:
The Gateway of Tears

Use this page to try your new sobriquets in a short piece of writing.

69

COFFEE-BREAK OBJECTS

Write an unexpected description of, or frame in an unusual context, some or all of the following objects you might see on your coffee break: coffee beans, cup, spoon, sugar packet, biscuit, plate, milk jug.

Example: Coffee and cream

{ "He was my cream, and I was his coffee—And when you poured us together, it was something."

Josephine Baker }

WATERY REFLECTIONS

Imagine a fictional character looking at a reflection in a pool of water, or musing while looking out to sea. Describe the scene, along with memories or longings for the future. How does the character feel in the moment?

EPIPHANY

Imagine a character who has an epiphany while sipping an afternoon mocha. Who are they? Where are they? What is their current life situation? What is their epiphany? How will their life change? You could write a story outline, a character profile, a short piece about the episode of the epiphany, or whatever fires your imagination.

72 FLIPPING PERSPECTIVES

A young person gives an aging homeless person a ham-and-cheese baguette and a cup of coffee. Write two accounts of an exchange between these two people: in one account have the homeless person be male and the young person female; then flip the sexes for the second account. Are there any subtle or drastic differences to the dynamic of the encounter? Do the voices change? Are there changes to the nuances of language during the exchange?

EXCHANGE 1
Homeless person: male
Young person: female

EXCHANGE 2

Homeless person: female
Young person: male

"When you have once seen the glow of happiness on the face of a beloved person, you know that a man can have no vocation but to awaken that light on the faces surrounding him. In the depth of winter, I finally learned that within me there lay an invincible summer."

Albert Camus

STORY GENERATION

"5 Whys" is an interrogative technique used to find the root cause of a problem, and can also be used for story generation. It is said that if the question "Why?" is applied to a problem, and answered "because...," then after five iterations of this questioning and answering, a root cause will be found.

One of the great plotline triggers in literature is for a character to be presented with a problem that must be overcome.

Using the page opposite, think of an initial problem that a character is compelled to overcome, and apply the 5 Whys method. Does this lead to a root cause and, consequently, story generation?

EXAMPLE

Problem:
A wife cannot find her husband.

1   Why? Because he has been kidnapped.

2   Why? Because his kidnappers want a ransom.

3   Why? Because the wife is a millionaire.

4   Why? Because the wife has potentially found a cure for cancer and is sponsored by a major pharmaceutical company.

5   Why? Because her kidnapped husband has cancer-fighting DNA.

PROBLEM

WHY 1? BECAUSE...

WHY 2? BECAUSE...

WHY 3? BECAUSE...

WHY 4? BECAUSE...

WHY 5? BECAUSE...

QUIRKS AND HABITS

Write down ten quirks, habits, or unique characteristics that might help to bring a character to life. Write a sentence or two for each of these quirks of character. For example, a woman has a pencil permanently propped behind her ear and a small notepad in her pocket:

"One hand reached for the pen, the other for her pocket. Her arms moved in perfect synchronization. For ten years she had never let a creative thought go unrecorded."

"My friends tried to ignore my quirks since they didn't have a clue what to do about them. It didn't seem hard on them though. They were already trained to ignore their parents' alcohol abuse, constant bickering, serial marriages, and nonsensical advice."

Terry Spencer Hesser, Kissing Doorknobs *(1999)*

75 MERGING CHARACTERS

Think of three of your favorite characters from literature, television, or the big screen. Write down some brief notes listing the key elements of their character, idiosyncrasies, and what motivates them.

CHARACTER 1

CHARACTER 2

CHARACTER 3

COMPOSITE CHARACTER

Now create a composite character, taking various elements from each of the characters opposite. As you make your sets of notes, do any new characters begin to emerge?

HISTORICAL EVENT

Write internal dialogue or an account from the perspective of somebody who has experienced, or is in the middle of, a famous historical event. Write directly from what you know of the event, beginning with some research notes, or make it up.

Use this space to jot down some notes: researched, remembered, or made up.

THE UNRELIABLE NARRATOR

Making it up and inferring details from what you think you might know makes you an "unreliable narrator." Such narration has been used to great effect in literature, from Aristophanes in the fifth century BCE to William Faulkner in the twentieth century. As readers, we are used to relying on narrators as an omnipresent witness, providing us with exact details of events within a story. This can be played with. The unreliable narrator can, for example, be used to create twists, taking us down one path only for truths to be revealed, leaving the reader to shift viewpoints.

DIFFERENT STYLES

77

"At breakfast the next day Page picked up a glass of what he thought was water. He spluttered to discover it was neat vodka."

Sebastian Faulks, The Fatal Englishman *(1996)*

Rewrite the extract above in three different styles. Choose from the following styles, or think of your own: poetic, monological, comedic, dramatic, romantic.

Style 1:

_____

_____

_____

_____

_____

Style 2:

_____

_____

_____

_____

Style 3:

_____

_____

_____

_____

_____

CAVEMAN COFFEE CUP

78

EVOLUTION
Explain to a caveman how your
coffee cup evolved.

79

LIFE HACKS

Write dialogue between two people exchanging life hacks (novel, clever, and innovative ways to speed up some of the everyday processes of life), such as using sunglasses to prop up your cell phone so that you can drink your coffee and eat a snack hands-free, the phone sitting on the frame of the glasses against the lenses, with arms crossed at the front to stop the phone from sliding to the table—"Wow, that was a lengthy description for a time-saving life hack!"

"The fact is that I don't know where ideas come from, or even where to look for them. Nor does any writer...the only real answer is to drink way too much coffee and buy yourself a desk that doesn't collapse when you beat your head against it."

Douglas Adams, The Salmon of Doubt: Hitchhiking the Galaxy One Last Time *(2005)*

HIDDEN SECRET

80

Write two or three brief character profiles below. Include their name, age, occupation, and where they live. Then take your characters and compose a few lines for each of them, exploring a hidden secret. You could write notes, a short narrative, or have them explain the secret in their own voice.

"Write what you know, and what do you know better than your own secrets?"

Raymond Carver

LOCATION VIEWPOINTS

In the boxes below, write down a specific location that you would be able to describe to somebody if meeting them there. Follow this by writing down three possible viewpoints of the location. This might be from above in a plane, from a boat in the sea looking toward land, from a passing train, etc.

Location

Viewpoint 1

Viewpoint 2

Viewpoint 3

In the boxes below, write a description of the location from each of the perspectives you have chosen.

Viewpoint 1: Description

Viewpoint 2: Description

Viewpoint 3: Description

THE LAST...

82

Write a single line to describe the following:

The last book you read

_____

_____

The last film you saw

_____

_____

The last vacation you went on

_____

_____

The last song you listened to

_____

_____

The last fact you heard

_____

_____

The last person you spoke to

_____

_____

"I go back to the reading room, where I sink down in the sofa and into the world of _The Arabian Nights_. Slowly, like a movie fadeout, the real world evaporates. I'm alone, inside the world of the story. My favorite feeling in the world."

Haruki Murakami, Kafka on the Shore (2002)

COHERENT PASSAGE

Can you rearrange the descriptions to form a coherent,
or semi-coherent, passage of writing? Use filler/link sentences
to tie the various elements together, where needed.

83 IDIOSYNCRATIC DIALOGUE

It is important to make dialogue sound real to the reader. Write an exchange between two people including some of the idiosyncrasies that show up in people's speech in the real world. Some examples are shown below.

EXAMPLES

1. Interrupting the person they are talking to, or themselves, with a sudden new thought.

2. Filler words, as they try to maintain their train of thought.

3. Any words of regional dialect or where their accent is particularly strong.

4. Hand movements and facial expressions that communicate without words.

SCENARIO IDEAS

• A couple splitting up

• Friends discussing politics

• Someone receiving a new witness protection identity

COMBINATIONS

Write down elements of nature, such as flowers, plants, rocks, and sky, along with their colors. Use these combinations to describe the color of something else.

For example:
"Chrysanthemum-purple mountainscape"
"Daffodil-yellow taxi"

NATURE
Elements of nature
and their color(s)

DESCRIPTIONS
Nature elements used to
describe something else

IN YOUR POCKET

Search your bag or pockets for an object you can take out. Describe it, and then continue to write about it, letting your imagination take you in any direction. It might be an old coin, where you muse over the places it has been, the people it has encountered, the items it has paid for.

DESCRIBING SENTIMENTS

 "Keep your face always toward the sunshine—and shadows will fall behind you."

Walt Whitman

This is a very novel and textured way to describe the idea of always remaining positive. Can you think of novel ways to outline the ethos behind one or all of the following sentiments?

ALWAYS REMAIN POSITIVE

NO REGRETS

REMAIN CALM UNDER PRESSURE

NEVER FEAR FAILURE

REVISITING SENTENCES

It can be interesting to look over your writing and find inspiration from it. Look back at some of your writing and copy four sentences from four previous exercises into the spaces below.

In the space below, compose a piece of writing using the previous sentences you have chosen, mixing up the order and adding new sentences to gel them together into something tangible. You may find your composition is slightly abstract. It is sure to be new and intriguing, and perhaps even highly readable, tangible, and exciting.

88

ONOMATOPOEIA

FIVE CATEGORIES

Onomatopoeic words imitate the sound they
describe, such as the word/sound BANG! Such words
fall into one of five categories: water (e.g., trickle),
air (e.g., swoosh), collisions (e.g., crash), voice (e.g.,
chatter), and animals (e.g., quack).

Write down some more examples
of your own onomatopoeic words
for each category:

WATER

AIR

COLLISIONS

VOICES

ANIMALS

"Plop, plop, fizz, fizz, oh what a relief it is."
Alka-Seltzer promotional campaign

Work your onomatopoeic words into sentences, a paragraph, or some lines of poetry.

_____

_____

_____

_____

_____

_____

_____

_____

_____

_____

_____

_____

_____

_____

_____

_____

_____

_____

_____

Beatrix Potter, who wrote the Peter Rabbit collection of children's books, invented new onomatopoeic words. We know the meaning from the sound they make, like a light, skipping motion: "After a time he began to wander about, going lippity-lippity not very fast, and looking all around." You might also like to make up some new unique onomatopoeic words.

89

SYMBOLISM

A useful tool to bring out hidden meanings, symbolism can also be a prelude to future events in a story. Below are some common examples of symbolism with the use of colors, objects, and flowers.

CONTINUE THIS PROCESS

Black—death

White—love, peace, purity

Red—passion, danger, immorality

Yellow—lack of courage

Chain—link between two things

Ladder—ascension to heaven

Broken mirror—separation

Roses—romance

Lilies—beauty, temptation

Can you think of other symbolic ideas? Can you come up with some of your own that you can use within your writing? Write them down along with any notes referring to how they might be used: scenarios, characters, dialogue. Alternatively, think how you might use some of the examples provided.

ON THE ROAD: SPONTANEITY

Write an account of when you were "on the road." In the space below, jot down a few key details, such as time, place, where you were headed, where you had left from, any people you met. Maybe you have a dramatic episode to recount, or just your feelings and observations as you traveled along a highway looking out of a car window as a child, stopping at a roadside diner, or on the way to where you are right now.

KEY DETAILS

JACK KEROUAC

Jack Kerouac (1922–1969) was an American autobiographical-novelist and poet who was at the forefront of the Beat Generation, writing with minimal editing. He wrote from personal experience of heavy drinking, drug taking, spirituality, travel, and jazz culture. Kerouac wrote in "spontaneous prose." He would often use a long connecting dash rather than a full stop. This acted as a method of keeping the pace and beat of his prose moving forward. When spoken, the dash acted more like a pause for breath than the grammatical end of a sentence. Kerouac's most famous work is *On the Road* (1957), a true-life account of his journey across America told by his alias, the narrator Sal Paradise.

Once you have some of the key elements nailed down, write in spontaneous prose without too much concern for grammar. Don't allow the process of correction or seeking total accuracy stem the flow of your writing. Consider using the long dash, rather than a full stop, like a pause for breath if you were speaking the words aloud.

SPONTANEOUS PROSE

91 A PHOTOGRAPH

Source a photograph—historical, infamous, or one of your own. Describe the photo with a basic description of what you see, and bring in other elements, such as your emotional response, memories, and insights. Perhaps create a story triggered by the image.

92

ART DIALOGUE

Think of a famous piece of artwork depicting people, such as David Hockney's *Mr and Mrs Clark and Percy* (1971) or Auguste Rodin's sculpture *The Thinker* (1904). Choose one or two people within the artwork and compose internal dialogue or a conversation between them.

93

FACING FEARS

Write down three of your biggest fears, or imagine three fears that a character of your choice might have.

FEAR 1

FEAR 2

FEAR 3

Write an episode in which a fictional character experiences an incident involving one or more of the fears you have listed on the previous page. If your character's biggest fear is heights, then you might have them teetering on the top of a tall building, edging away from a pointed gun, trying to talk their way to safety.

WHAT IF?

94

Write a very short story or a plot outline using the "What if?" scenarios below. Alternatively, come up with a scenario of your own.

WHAT IF...you open your bedroom blinds in the morning and the world outside is completely unrecognizable to you?

WHAT IF...the car you are driving begins to drive itself?

WHAT IF...nobody else in the world wakes from their sleep except you?

95

MAGICAL REALISM

Write a short piece about a magical episode that occurs in a place far removed from the magical, like a busy open market, a roadhouse, or a dog track.

MAKING THE MAGIC REAL

Magical realism is where magical elements are brought into a real-life situation. It is important to keep the language in your prose as mundane, nondescript, and realistic as possible. The desired effect is to make the magic appear believable by framing it in a real-life setting. One of the great modern examples of this genre is *One Hundred Years of Solitude* (1967) by Gabriel García Márquez.

96

TORN LETTER

Compose a snippet of writing inside the torn piece of paper opposite, imagining that it has been ripped away from the end of a letter.

Use the space below to write who the letter is to and from, the period it was written (e.g., modern day or many years ago), and the general subject of the letter. Alternatively, just wing it and write directly into the torn paper the words and sentiments at the end of an imagined letter, allowing the protagonists and time period to emerge and evolve as you write.

NOTE BOX

CHARACTER PROFILE: LAYERS

Write a character profile starting with a basic knowledge of their personality and appearance. Then add a second layer describing their work life and relationships. A third layer should detail any habits and idiosyncrasies that are personal to the character. Finish with a final layer of information only you as the writer and they as the character know: What is their fifth-favorite Christmas movie? Which song comes into their head every Monday morning when they take a shower? How did they celebrate when they taught their dog to high-five? Delve into the character and keep going until you know them inside out—what drives them, what keeps them awake at night.

FIRST LAYER
Personality/appearance

SECOND LAYER
Work life/relationships

THIRD LAYER
Habits/idiosyncrasies

FINAL LAYER
Secret information

98

LEARNING FROM LIFE

Imagine your character on each of the prominent birthdays listed on the opposite page. Write a sentence or two about what they have learnt in the years since their previous birthday. How do their thoughts and character change as they grow older? What might have happened in their life between each birthday to affect their outlook? Write a short character profile using the prompts below.

CHARACTER PROFILE

Name:

Sex:

Country of birth:

Country of residence:

Education:

Profession(s):

10 YEARS _____

_____

_____

_____

21 YEARS _____

_____

_____

_____

30 YEARS _____

_____

_____

_____

50 YEARS _____

_____

_____

_____

70 YEARS _____

_____

_____

_____

99 LYRICAL DESCRIPTIONS

In the box headed "Sounds," write down five words used to describe a sound. In the box headed "Nature," write down five words relating to the natural world. Then, form pairs of words, combining the two categories. Create some sentences using these lyrical descriptions in the larger box below.

SOUNDS
e.g., Vibration

NATURE
e.g., Trees

LYRICAL SENTENCES
e.g., The trees vibrated as the chainsaw moved closer.

100 CHILDHOOD MEMORIES

In the box below, write down three sounds and three songs that return you to your childhood.

Take these childhood memories and compose a short piece of writing from the perspective of a character situated in one of the following locations: the top of a mountain, the edge of a jungle, the middle of the ocean.

ACKNOWLEDGMENTS

Page	IMAGE CREDITS
27	Tiwat K, shutterstock
32	Tiwat K, shutterstock
39	Lermot, shutterstock
48	nikiteev_konstantin, shutterstock
60	AVS-Images, shutterstock
60	nikiteev_konstantin, shutterstock
68	nikiteev_konstantin, shutterstock
97	Lermot, shutterstock
100–101	Claire Munday
115	Lermot, shutterstock
169	AVS-Images, shutterstock

Page	ADDITIONAL QUOTE SOURCES

If the source information is not listed below the quote it can be found below.

33	goodreads.com/quotes/52790
53	goodreads.com/quotes/132400
59	goodreads.com/quotes/142425
61	goodreads.com/quotes/172515
80	Story attributed to Ernest Hemingway in *Peter Miller's Get Published! Get Produced!* *(1991)* Attribution repeated in a letter by Arthur C. Clarke published by Robert Colombo in 1992
92	goodreads.com/quotes/4832
99	penguinrandomhouse.ca/books/32504/generation-a-by-douglas-coupland/9780307357731
124	goodreads.com/quotes/24289
129	goodreads.com/quotes/226128
142	goodreads.com/quotes/945593
152	brainyquote.com/citation/quotes/walt_whitman_384665
156	thoughtco.com/onomatapoeia-word-sounds-1691451